THE '9Fs' BR's HEAVY FREIGHT LOCOMOTIVES

JOHN SCOTT MORGAN & MARINA KNIFE

IAN ALLAN Publishing

Dedication

This book is dedicated to the memory of Richard Martino; steam engineer, preservationist and restorer of all things steam, craftsman and artist. A greatly missed friend who died on 15 June 1992 as a result of a boiler accident on the steam yacht *Corolla* at Bucklers Hard, Hampshire.

Also in memory of Tom Martino, his nephew aged 15, who also died as a result of the same accident.

Acknowledgements

I should like to thank the following people for their kindness and enthusiastic assistance in the production of this book:

David Shepherd for kindly writing the afterword to this book and for having the foresight to save the first privately preserved '9F' 2-10-0, No 92203; *Ron White* of Colour Rail for allowing me free access to his exemplary library of railway images; *Bert Collins* for his narrative on the '9F Experience', which gives a graphic account of these fine locomotives, probably for the first time in print. I should like to reserve a special thank you to *Marina Knife* for transcribing raw notes into the book you now read. I would like to acknowledge the following photographers for the use of their slides: *C. J. Gammell; G. T. Robinson; R. Ives* and *M. Mensing*.

Bibliography

'9F' Locomotives, Locoprofiles, the late Brian Reed; *The British '9F' 2-10-0s*, Irwell Press, P. Atkins; *The Standard Steam Locomotives of British Railways*, David & Charles, R. P. Bradley.

First published 1994

ISBN 0 7110 2265 8

© Ian Allan Ltd 1994

Designed by Alan C. Butcher

Published by Ian Allan Publishing

an imprint of Ian Allan Ltd, Terminal House, Station Approach, Shepperton, Surrey TW17 8AS; and printed by Ian Allan Printing Ltd, Coombelands House, Coombelands Lane, Addlestone, Weybridge, Surrey KT15 1HY.

Introduction

The final design of the '9F' 2-10-0s was derived from original proposals and specifications drawn up for heavy freight locomotives designated type 90. First envisaged by E. S. Cox, R. C. Bond and Robin Riddles in 1948, as 2-8-2 locomotives, the '9F' 2-10-0 heavy freight locomotives were one of the last designs to appear from the Brighton Drawing Office.

It was decided that the 2-8-2 wheel arrangement would not provide the adhesion required for heavy freight locomotives. Therefore, the concept was changed to that of a 2-10-0. The Class 9F, as the type became known, was probably the least conventional in construction of parts and fittings within the standard type locomotives, designed and built by British Railways.

The weight in working order of a standard locomotive was 86ton 14cwt; tender weight ranged from 50ton 5cwt to 55ton 5cwt depending on type; with a boiler pressure of 250lb/square inch, outside cylinders at 20in x 28in, giving a tractive effort of 39,667lb. The driving wheels were 5ft 0in diameters with centrecoupled wheels flangeless. Pony wheels 3ft 0in overall, overall length 66ft 2in with Walschaerts valve gear.

The class was built between 1954 and 1960, with construction divided between the British Railways workshops at Crewe and Swindon — Crewe constructed 178 machines against Swindon's 73 machines, a total of 251 locomotives being built, over a six year period.

Previous page:
No 92215 showing signs of neglect works a fitted freight through Lapworth in the summer of 1965. Note the missing smokebox number plate. Built at Swindon in 1959 and first allocated to Banbury, it was withdrawn from Wakefield in 1967. Seen here with a BR1G tender. *M. Mensing*

Front cover:
Through the winter snow, No 92031 wheels an up mineral train, passing Charwelton in March 1963. These trains were a feature of the Great Central from prewar days until the mid-1960s, when freight was diverted away from the GC main line. *M. Mensing*

The '9F' class locomotives were paired with five types of British Railways tenders. These were of varying water capacity and designated to different regional areas as follows: BR1B water capacity 4,725gal NER and LMR; BR1C water capacity 4,725gal LMR; BR1F water capacity 5,625gal ER; BR1G water capacity 5,000gal WR; and BR1K water capacity 4,325gal LMR. The latter were used exclusively for the three mechanical stoker-fitted locomotives which ran on LMR. The locomotives fitted with the Franco Crosti boilers were also paired with BR1B tenders.

Operationally, the class was divided between the main regions, with the exception of the Southern and Scottish Regions, which had small numbers of the class working over their metals for short periods only. The Southern Region had a small batch of '9Fs'; based at Eastleigh they worked the Fawley oil trains over the Didcot, Newbury & Southampton line for a short time in the early 1960s.

The Scottish Region ran a series of trials with the '9F' class in the early 1960s. However, no members of the class were permanently sent north of the border as a result of these trials. The Scottish Region was well served by 20 of the Riddles War Department 2-10-0s.

The main allocation of '9F' locomotives was as follows: Western 56, London Midland 100, Eastern 85 and North Eastern 10.

Ten '9F' locomotives fitted with Franco Crosti boilers were allocated to the London Midland Region's Midland main line for working heavy coal traffic from the Nottingham and Lancashire coalfields to London.

Without a doubt, the '9F' design was one of the best modern postwar locomotive types built in Britain, even taking into account both the other standard types built by British Railways, or the machines built in Britain, specifically for export at this time.

A number of experiments were carried out, including the fitting of Berkley mechanical stokers to three machines, Nos 92165/6/7. Also No 92250 was fitted with a very successful Giesl ejector in 1960, although this was not extended to other members of the '9F' class.

The 10 locomotives fitted with Franco Crosti boilers were less successful than the other members of the class. This group were all eventually converted to conventional operation by the early 1960s. As a result of the 'rebuilding', which retained the smaller non-standard boiler, there was a loss in the overall weight of each locomotive and this in actual terms technically made them '8Fs'; the difference being 4.55ton less in adhesive weight, 6.6ton less in total.

'9F' No 92079 was fitted with a large headlight from the ex-Midland Railway 0-10-0 'Big Bertha', and put to work on the Lickey Incline, being stationed at Bromsgrove in the late 1950s and early 1960s. When this locomotive was away for repairs, or overhaul, it would take up to four '94xx' pannier tanks to do the same work.

Left:
A lightly weathered No 92233 heads up the bank at Masbury on the 9.25am Bournemouth-Crewe on 18 August 1962. The '9Fs' were normally loaned by a number of Western Region sheds to the S&D section to cover the summer traffic and proved very successful for these duties. Built at Crewe in 1958, first allocated to Pontypool Road and withdrawn from Speke Junction in 1968. Seen here with a BR1G tender. *Colour-Rail*

The Class 9F 2-10-0s found favour as passenger locomotives within the same period. Members were used on passenger service on the Somerset & Dorset, the Great Central and for a brief period on the Western Region, operating mostly on the Paddington and South Wales line, including heading the 'Red Dragon' on a number of occasions.

Fate decreed that the last steam locomotive built for British Railways was to be a '9F', this being No 92220; named *Evening Star* at Swindon by Keith Grand, General Manager of the Western Region in March 1960. No 92220 was the only member officially named, and also the only member of the class to receive lined passenger green livery.

The '9Fs' design had a beauty far surpassing other modern types built for similar work in foreign countries. These fine and beautiful machines deserved better than to be mere freight locomotives. Considering their ability and outstanding performance record on all kinds of work, perhaps the design should have been designated for mixed traffic.

Tragically, the '9F' locomotives were one of the many victims in the 1955 'modernisation plan', and therefore were withdrawn due to rapid dieselisation and electrification, years before their time. No attempts whatsoever were made to sell these fine locomotives to possible foreign buyers. One consideration could have been Turkey, as they possessed a compatible modern standard gauge steam locomotive fleet. The last members of the class were withdrawn in June 1968, only a month and a half before the end of steam.

The nearest European design was the German DR/DB Class 52 and 52UK 2-10-0, of which 6,100 examples were built, both during and after World War 2. Robin Riddles designed an earlier austerity type 2-10-0 for the War Department in 1942, along with a 2-8-0 design during the same period. The WD 2-10-0 was, however, very different in design and concept to the '9F' 2-10-0, lacking in the refinements that made the '9F' a well received and well loved design.

There are nine members of the class preserved and the locations are as follows: Nos 92134 Sail & Steam Engineering, Brightlingsea; 92203 East Somerset Railway (now named *Black Prince*); 92207 East Lancs Railway (to be named *Morning Star*); 92212 Great Central Railway; 92214 and 92219 both at Midland Railway Centre; 92220 *Evening Star* National Railway Museum, York; 92240 Bluebell Railway and 92245 Bute Town Historical Railway Centre.

Left:
No 92001 passing Moorewood on the 10.32am Bournemouth-Manchester in August 1962. This scene has a number of features which include an interesting formation of mixed carriage stock with a Gresley brake third at the head of the train. The rest of the formation consists of Mk 1 stock and more Gresley vehicles at the rear of the train. Other points include the S&D lower quadrant signal of LSWR origin, and the abandoned sidings.
Colour-Rail/J. P. Mullett (SD68)

Right:
No 92154 makes its way out of Woodford Halse with a Bradford-Poole train on 29 August 1964. Passing a fine array of LNER bracket upper quadrant signals, the train formation consists of a mixture of former LMS and GW vehicles with some BR Mk 1 stock. Built at Crewe in 1957, allocated to Toton, withdrawn from Warrington in 1967 and fitted with a BR1C tender. *Colour-Rail*

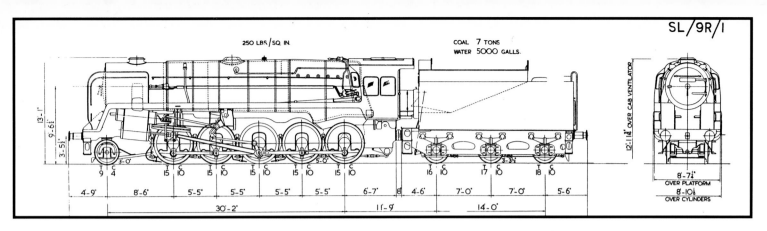

250 LBS./SQ. IN.

COAL 7 TONS
WATER 5000 GALLS.

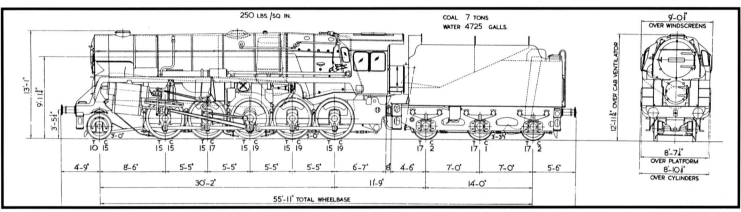

250 LBS./SQ. IN.

COAL 7 TONS
WATER 4725 GALLS.

55'-11" TOTAL WHEELBASE

Top:
BR Standard Class 9F 2-10-0.

Above:
Franco Crosti-boilered version
as built.

5

The '9F' Experience

Bert Collins

There is little doubt that the arrival of the '9Fs' on the Peterboro'-London heavy goods and mineral services provided the next best thing to the long awaited diesels that many locomotive men had yearned for.

Hitherto, heavy goods had been in the hands of a variety of six- and eight-coupled engines, of numerous classes, none of which ever found much favour with locomen.

For a half century or so, each class from the GNR 'Long Toms' of 1901, right through to the 'Austerity' 2-8-0s of 1943 made footplate work, at times, highly disagreeable.

At Hornsey, where I was a fireman, there had always been a mistrust of 'big engines'. After all, that shed's allocation nearly always consisted of 70-odd small six-coupled tank engines with a few tender engines. Hornsey men had had

experience of work on the Gresley 'P1' 2-8-2s (or 'Boosters' as they were known). But these two engines were arguably the two most detested engines ever to work between Peterborough and London, mainly due to heavily clinkering fires, blocked ashpans and consequent steaming problems, which were exacerbated by stops for long periods at signals on goods lines whilst they awaited a clearance path on to the main line. Happily, for me, these engines had gone when I joined the railway!

As a general rule, coal trains of exceptional length were kept to the main line rather than via the Hertford loop, due not only to the short sections between Cuffley and Bowes Park, but also because of the rollercoaster nature of the line and the real threat of coupling snatch and the consequent risk of

breaking loose — a situation which prevailed until the end of World War 2.

During this period, the Gresley 2-8-0s which had virtually monopolised heavy freight work between the wars were retired to less exacting duties elsewhere, and their work passed to the 'Austerity' 2-8-0s. This was where I came in.

I joined the LNER at the back end of 1947 as a cleaner at King's Cross, Top Shed. When I passed the test to become a fireman, I decided that it made sense to work at Hornsey Loco, rather than King's Cross, my home at that time being a 15 minute walk from Hornsey shed. As I progressed through the various links, I gained much experience with 'Austerities', 'K3s' and 'V2s', as the result of changing turns with firemen who preferred a more leisurely way to spend their eight hours. Over the years, much has been written on British locomotive matters and many have chronicled the rough riding of the 'K3s'. It is true that there were rogue members of this class, but the rough riding characteristics that we have heard about have, in many cases, been exaggerated and although they were

at times rough, I have nothing but affection for the 'K3s'. These same writers had obviously never had a trip on a well worn 'Austerity'!

To say austerities engines rode rough is to understate. The boiler tended to move from side to side between the frame as the cab sides oscillated vertically and the floor juddered, whilst the tender buffeted against the cab drag beam. All these factors combined to make footplate work extremely uncomfortable. There were many trips on these unfortunate engines before salvation for us arrived in the shape of the '9Fs'.

Demand for coal from both industrial and domestic users began to decline. It thus followed that it became necessary to shorten coal trains and this process had started just before the arrival of the '9Fs'. Very often we would work up with a short 44-wagon coal train, which had been marshalled as far north as Colwick. In fact, this type of train formed two southbound London trains, only requiring a mid-train split on arrival at Ferme Park, Hornsey. The result was that coal transit time was speeded up quite considerably. It became noticeable that the sidings at Ferme Park became less congested, not only as a result of steadily declining traffic, but also because of sharper working practices.

With the advent of the '9Fs' train operation took on a new look. Instead of New England and Hornsey crews changing over at Hitchin in order to avoid excessive overtime, it became possible for single crews to work coal trains and return empties throughout.

Far left:
No 92168 leaves York shed under a pall of smoke. Built at Crewe in 1957 and first allocated to Doncaster, it is seen here paired to a BR1F tender. The locomotive was withdrawn from Doncaster in 1965. One of the first withdrawals of the class on the Eastern Region. *Colour-Rail*

Left:
'9F' in profile under the roof at Birmingham New Street in 1958. This unidentified member of the class with a single chimney stands in the afternoon sun. *M. Mensing*

As already mentioned, in the past Hornsey men did not take too kindly to 'big engines'. With the arrival of the '9Fs', there was a deal of uneasiness until the men became fully acclimatised and then they never looked back. The initial allocation of '9Fs' to New England were Nos 92011, 92030-40. They were soon put into traffic and proved very popular, generally becoming known as 'Spaceships'.

Locomen worked to three criteria. Did the engine steam? Was the riding comfortable? Would the engine be capable of fulfilling its diagrammed duties? The '9Fs' scored high marks on all counts. After the spartan facilities offered on previous classes, it was a pleasure to be able to carry out much of one's work whilst seated. The fireman's controls were conveniently situated in front of him, which was not only more comfortable, but from a safety viewpoint also allowed the fireman more opportunity to keep a good look out. As the men became used to the '9Fs', it reached a stage at the shed whereby enginemen left no one in any doubt as to their feelings if they found an 'Austerity' number against their name when they signed on for duty!

By 1954, I had graduated to Hornsey's main line goods link where I was rostered with Driver Charles Barnes. Charlie and I developed a good relationship from the start. We both liked to work on a clean footplate. By its very nature, of course, the operation of a steam locomotive was a messy business, but with good preparation at the shed, it was possible to clean and hose the footplate down. Then, after a good wash, using a bucket of hot water from the engine, we left the shed and we were always able to keep ourselves reasonably clean. At the shed, I always made a fairly heavy fire up at the back end of the grate of a '9F', which would give us a good start if we were likely to leave Ferme Park with an 80-wagon train.

One snag with the '9Fs' was the problem of glare from the firehole at night. Because of the shallow slope of the backhead into the cab, drivers experienced serious difficulties in sighting semaphore signals. In an attempt to alleviate this problem, No 92011 was fitted with a Class V2-type firehole door as an experiment, the idea being that we could fire through the door flap in the traditional GN manner. The trouble was that the already mentioned shallow angle of the backhead meant that the firehole flap was set at a downward angle, making it

impossible to deliver coal to all areas of the grate. The problem of glare did persist, but we found it helped if I fired the engine right-handed, ie: with my back to the driver, rather than by the usual left-handed method. Charlie always allowed me to have the regulator during the day as he enjoyed firing and it gave him useful exercise. Charlie treated the firing of a locomotive as an art form. His limited firing experience with wide fireboxes was on the Class P1 2-8-2s, but at the age of 62 he could still swing a shovelful of coal with consummate ease. His seniority dated from 1912 when GNR drivers were on a fuel economy bonus scheme, and Charlie's method still applied these techniques. Every shovelful was destined for a precise place in the grate. Never too heavy a fire, but one which would provide plenty of steam with the minimum coal and effort.

I can remember one particular week when a Peterborough driver was learning the road with us over the Hertford loop. The weather was hot and I decided that, with three of us on the engine, it would be preferable if the minimum amount of firing was done. I therefore decided to fill the firebox up. We reached Hitchin without me having to touch the fire once. Charlie never spoke to me for a week! I thought there goes my driving turns, but before long we had made it up and I was soon back at the regulator. Needless to say, I never did a firebox fill up again!

With the '9Fs' I can never remember the use of full regulator, despite having loads of up to 65 wagons of loaded coal or 80 return empties. With a powerful steam brake and a fair turn of foot, we were able to find more frequent paths between passenger trains and in particular over the Hertford loop.

New England was never noted for its maintenance of freight engines, and this applied equally to the '9Fs', but it seemed to make little difference to them, unlike the horrors that we endured with the 'Austerities'.

There is little doubt that working the '9Fs' had made footplate work on heavy freight duties a pleasure. Small wonder then that as more engines of the class became available they found themselves on more exacting duties, including the occasional express passenger train where they gave a very good account of themselves.

After half a century with engines that, for a number of reasons, found disfavour with the men who had to work them, it was ironic that once the ultimate steam locomotives had arrived, their life span should have been such a short one.

Somerset & Dorset '9Fs'

'9F' No 92001 passing Midsomer Norton South on the 9.53am Bath-Bournemouth service in August 1962. The train strikes a marked contrast against the summer flowers with the rake of maroon Stanier carriage stock. Built at Crewe in 1954, first allocated to Ebbw Junction and finally withdrawn from Wakefield in 1967. Seen here with a BRIG tender. *Colour-Rail/J. P. Mullett (SD67)*

No 92209 takes water at Blandford Forum in February 1964, with the South Western Rambler rail tour. The carriage stock is of interest with a mixture of Maunsell Restriction 1 and Bulleid stock. The Maunsell stock was rapidly being withdrawn at this time, and this was probably one of the last rail tours that featured this stock. Built at Swindon in 1959, first allocated to Laira and finally withdrawn from Bristol Barrow Road in 1965. Seen here with BR1G tender. *Colour-Rail*

No 92233 heads up Masbury Summit on the 7.25pm Bournemouth-Crewe in August 1962. Although this train and locomotive have been featured before, this picture shows the rake of Stanier Corridor stock to great effect. *Colour-Rail/J. P. Mullett (SD71)*

Left:
Halted at signals No 92245 stands at Templecombe Junction, August 1962. The '9F', its safety valves lifted, ferociously releases steam against a stormy black sky. This photograph shows both the bracket signals to great advantage. Built at Crewe in 1958, first allocated to Old Oak Common, and withdrawn from Southall in 1964. Seen here with a BR1G.
Colour-Rail/J. G. Dewing (SD128)

Above:
The last 'Pines Express' headed by No 92220 *Evening Star* at Evercreech Junction in September 1962. After watering, the classic passenger-green liveried locomotive draws the last down train into history.
Colour-Rail/B. J. Harding (SD197)

13

Southern Visiting '9F' 2-10-0s

Ex-works '9F' No 92231 at Eastleigh shed on 26 May 1963. A small number of the class were allocated to the Southern Region at this time, being used on heavy freight and oil trains over the Didcot, Newbury & Southampton line. The allocation ended in 1964. Built at Crewe in 1958, first allocated to Pontypool Road and finally withdrawn from York in 1966. Seen here with a BR1G tender. *Colour-Rail*

After hauling an inter-regional freight from the London Midland Region, a rusty and ash-covered No 92184 stands at the head of a line of 'dead' locomotives at Feltham shed on 8 November 1964. Built at Swindon in 1958 and first allocated to New England, being withdrawn from Immingham in 1965. Seen here with a BRIF tender.
Colour-Rail

'9Fs' in service

Above:
Drifting through Leicester Central on 31 August 1961, No 92010 heads an unfitted train of mineral wagons. Judging by the 2-10-0's overall condition, this locomotive is probably in need of some attention. Note the saline stains down the boiler cladding sheets, both at the front and firebox end, from the top feed and washout plugs. Great Central stations were of a grand nature usually with vast island platforms and beautiful buildings. Note the unusual broken white lines along the platform edge, a GC feature in British Rail days. Built at Crewe in 1954 and first allocated to March, being withdrawn from Kingmoor and seen here with a BR1F tender.
Colour-Rail

Right:
'9F', 'Spaceship', No 92067 emerges into the evening sunshine from Catesby tunnel with an up freight on 10 September 1961, its rust and dirt stained form contrasting against the bleached yellow grass in the background. The first wagon behind the tender is an original Ministry of Supply wartime built 16ton mineral wagon — an earlier version of the standard BR 16ton short wheelbase mineral wagon, built in their thousands after 1948. No 92067 was built at Crewe in 1955, first allocated to Doncaster and finally withdrawn from Kingmoor in 1966. Seen here with a BR1F tender.
Colour-Rail

Below:
Against a blue autumn sky, No 92093 heads its train of 16ton minerals out of Catesby on an up train. This photograph, taken on 10 September 1961, typifies the type of heavy mineral traffic to be found at this time on the Great Central section. This traffic was taken away from the GC for political reasons in 1965, to help to justify the closure of this valuable route. Built at Crewe in 1957, first allocated to Doncaster and finally withdrawn from Kingmoor in 1967. Seen here with a BR1F tender.
Colour-Rail

Right:
Western Region '9F' No 92001 at Banbury, in almost ex-works condition, on 9 September 1964. This photograph shows the fine features of these beautiful locomotives, with their slender boiler design, double chimney and impressive 10-coupled wheel sets. This locomotive was built at Crewe and outshopped on 12 January 1954, being allocated to the Western Region in February 1954. It is paired with a BR1G tender; later this was replaced with a BR1F tender.
Colour-Rail

Left:
'9F' in the sunset, No 92118 prepares to start its freight train out of Banbury in September 1964. The warm yellow rays of evening sun glint across the long boiler barrel and cabside of the '9F', as the locomotive crew look back for the signal from the guard. Built at Crewe in 1956, first allocated to Westhouses and finally withdrawn from Carnforth in 1968. Seen here with a BR1C tender.
Colour-Rail

Above:
No 92180 is seen at Woolmer Green hauling a rake of mineral wagons on 22 September 1962. Built in November 1957, No 92180 was initially allocated to New England shed. Withdrawn in April 1965 from Langwith shed, the locomotive had a working life of less than eight years.
Colour-Rail

Above:
The last Tyne Dock-Consett mineral train ran on 16 November 1966. Hauled by '9F' No 92063, which was specially cleaned and painted up to work this service, seen here while running light at Tyne Dock. This marked the end of these trains which were worked by the 10 '9Fs' allocated to the North Eastern Region and it also marked the end of '9F' operation in the northeast of England. No 92063 was built in Crewe in 1955 and was first allocated to Tyne Dock from where it was withdrawn in 1966. It is seen here with a BR1B tender. *Colour-Rail*

Right:
Ex-works at Darlington, No 92181 stands in the works yard, on 14 August 1960. This single chimney Swindon-built '9F' is paired with a BRIF tender. Built at Swindon in 1957, first allocated to New England and withdrawn from there in 1965. Note the WD 2-8-0 behind, also ex-works and awaiting dispatch back to its home shed. *Colour-Rail*

Below:
Working light after a mineral turn, No 92060 heads out across the junction at Tyne Dock on 7 April 1964. The 10 North Eastern Region '9Fs' were fitted with air pumps to work the automatic doors on the mineral wagons used on the Tyne Dock-Consett trains. Built at Crewe in 1955 and first allocated to Wellingborough it was finally withdrawn from Tyne Dock in 1966 and is seen here with a BRIC tender. *Colour-Rail*

Right:
Western Region '9F' in the afternoon sun, No 92241 stands in the yard at Woodford Halse in April 1962. It was built at Crewe in 1958, entering traffic in October of that year at Ebbw Junction. The locomotive served most of its life on the Western Region before being withdrawn from Southall in 1965. No 92241 was paired all its life with a BR1G tender, as shown in this photograph.
Colour-Rail//J. B. Hall (BRE1111)

Left:
Blasting up the grade near Stanley with a train of 20ton hopper wagons for Consett, '9F' No 92064 leads its heavy load towards the summit, leaving a cloud of black claggy smoke in its wake. No 92064 was built at Crewe in 1955; initially being allocated to Wellingborough on loan, and then Toton before finally being sent to Tyne Dock in May 1956, from where it was withdrawn in 1966.
Colour-Rail/J. D. Gomersall (BRE609)

Below:
A working portrait of No 92099, with black smoke rising from its single chimney as it passes South Pelaw, with a train of 21ton coal hoppers in July 1966. The locomotive has an oily clean look, its smokebox door hinges and locking handles are picked out in white paint. Even at this late date some Tyne Dock crews took extra interest in and care of their machines. No 92099 was built at Crewe in 1956, initially being sent to Tyne Dock from where it was withdrawn in 1966. The locomotive is shown here with a BR1B tender which it ran with all its life.
Colour-Rail/J. D. Gomersall (BRE609)

In the morning sunlight, No 92216 stands in the shed yard at Cardiff Canton in June 1960, surrounded by 'Castle' and 'Hall' class locomotives. No 92216 was built at Swindon in 1959, and completed all its service on the Western Region, its first shed being Cardiff Canton, the last being Severn Tunnel Junction, from where it was withdrawn in 1965.
Colour-Rail

In the winter of 1965, No 92128 heads a train of 16ton mineral wagons up Hatton Bank, leaving a trail of white steam in its wake. Built at Crewe in 1957, it was first allocated to Toton and finally withdrawn from Carnforth in 1967. It is paired here with a BR1C tender. *M. Mensing*

Left:
No 92212 makes its way through a green flank cutting near Harbury in the summer of 1965, with a mixed freight train made up of vans and other odd wagons. Note the long wheelbased standard BR tank wagon, the third vehicle behind the locomotive. Built at Crewe in 1959, No 92212 was allocated to Banbury and was withdrawn from Carnforth in 1968; seen here with a BR1F tender.
M. Mensing

Above:
Caught easing its train of Mk 1 stock into Oxford station on 31 July 1965, No 92001 passes a fine Great Western bracket signal. Built at Crewe in 1954, No 92001 was the second member of the class and was allocated to the Western Region from the time it entered traffic. The locomotive was later transferred via Tyseley to the London Midland Region, being withdrawn from Wakefield shed in 1967. It has a BR1G tender in this photograph.
Colour-Rail

A clean and well kept No 92060 nears Penton Junction with a train of empty bogie bolster flats in June 1963. This photograph shows the air pump equipment, a feature of the 10 '9F' locomotives allocated to the North Eastern Region. This single chimney '9F' has a BR1B tender. No 92060 was built at Crewe in 1955, entering traffic at Tyne Dock, being loaned to Wellingborough in the same year. It was withdrawn from service at Tyne Dock in 1966. *Colour-Rail*

No 92166, fitted with an American-designed Berkley mechanical stoker, outside the Rugby test plant. Evaluation tests were carried out at Rugby to assess the advantages of mechanical firing, these taking place during the winter of 1958 and the following spring. Built at Crewe in 1958, then allocated for a brief period to Saltley prior to the tests, No 92166 was finally withdrawn from Birkenhead in 1967. Although not in this picture, No 92166 ran with a BR1K tender.
Colour-Rail/National Railway Museum

No 92158 on shed at Cricklewood on 28 May 1963, surrounded by
Stanier '8F' 2-8-0s. Built at Crewe in 1957, this locomotive was first
sent to Toton and withdrawn from Speke Junction in 1966. No
92158 is paired with a BRIC tender with which it ran all its working
life. *Colour-Rail*

Saved for preservation, No 92203 and Standard Class 4 4-6-0, No 75029 near Chiltern Green on the journey from Crewe to the Longmoor Military Railway via Cricklewood in March 1968. No 92203 was built at Swindon in 1959 and was first allocated to St Philip's Marsh shed, being withdrawn from Birkenhead in 1967. It ran all its working life with a BR1G tender and was later named *Black Prince* whilst No 75029 was named *Green Knight*. Both locomotives were purchased by David Shepherd (the wildlife artist) for ultimate use on the East Somerset Railway.
Colour-Rail

Left:
No 92156 in the shed yard at Willesden on 27 June 1964, alongside Stanier '8F' 2-8-0s awaiting their next turn of duty. No 92156 was built at Crewe in 1957, allocated to Toton and later transferred to Warrington, from where it was withdrawn in 1967. It was paired with a BR1C tender.
Colour-Rail

Above:
Nos 92113 and 92077 at Wellingborough on 6 May 1963. Wellingborough was a main shed for members of the class from the mid-1950s, quite apart from the Franco Crosti examples. There were a sizeable number of single and double chimney '9Fs' allocated there. Nos 92113 and 92077 were Crewe-built, both being outshopped in 1956. No 92113 was first allocated to Westhouses, being withdrawn from Birkenhead in 1967; it was paired with a BR1C tender. No 92077, first sent to Toton and withdrawn from Carnforth in 1968, has a BR1F tender.
Colour-Rail

Left:
On a bright warm spring morning, No 92070 works a train of hoppers past a Midland Railway wooden-posted lower quadrant signal on its journey through the Peak District in March 1965. This single chimney '9F' was built at Crewe in 1956, first being sent to Doncaster and withdrawn from Birkenhead in 1967. It is paired with a BR1F tender. *Colour-Rail/J. B. Snell (BRM1105)*

Below:
With the backdrop of a blue sky and mountains beyond No 92017 crosses Ais Gill viaduct, with a train of long wheelbased 21ton hoppers in September 1965. No 92017 was built at Crewe in 1954, first being allocated to Wellingborough and withdrawn from Carlisle Kingmoor in 1967. It is paired with a BR1C tender. *Colour-Rail/A. E. R. Cope (BRM536)*

Pulling a train of 21ton hoppers with ease, No 92019 rides the bank south of Blea Moor tunnel in June 1965. The bleak grassland of the Settle & Carlisle line and the grey dry stone walling along the lineside contrasts with the dirty black '9F'. No 92019 was built at Crewe in 1954 and first allocated to Wellingborough, to be finally withdrawn from Carlisle Kingmoor in 1967. It has a BR1C tender. *Colour-Rail/A. Sainty Collection (BRM742)*

No 92125 pulls a mixed freight train near Shap Wells in the summer of 1964. The train has an interesting make-up, with examples of loaded container flats painted and lettered in the mid-1960s rail freight livery. Note the banker at the rear of the train, a common sight on these freight trains. No 92125 was built at Crewe in 1957, first allocated to Wellingborough and withdrawn from Carlisle in 1967. It has a BR1C tender.
Colour-Rail/A. E. R. Cope

Passing Kelmarsh Box, with a train of ironstone 12ton opens, No 92078 makes light work of a long heavy mineral train in September 1964. This is an attractive scene with the LNWR signalbox in its gulf red and cream paint and LMS upper quadrant bracket signal in the background. No 92078 was built at Crewe in 1956 being allocated to Toton and withdrawn from service at Warrington in 1967. It is paired with a BR1F tender.
Colour-Rail/(BRM1364)T. Tomalin

Big, black and beautiful, No 92088 hauling a train of 12ton mineral wagons loaded with chalk in October 1961. The train is at Weedon and about to go down the branch to Daventry. This stunning photograph is one of the finest images in the book, showing a '9F' in mint condition. No 92088 was built at Swindon in 1956, first allocated to Doncaster and finally withdrawn from Carnforth in 1968. It has a BR1F tender.
Colour-Rail

Left inset:
Blazing through the snow, its drain cocks open, No 92182 blasts its way down the tracks, and the powdery snow away from under its wheels and cylinders, passing Swayfield on 23 December 1963. The locomotive was built at Swindon in 1957, being allocated first to New England depot and withdrawn from Doncaster in 1966. Seen here with a BR1F tender.
Colour-Rail

Left:
Soot blackened No 92249 leaves Carlisle with an up train of soda ash tanks in October 1966. This type of traffic during this period was, for the most part, worked by '9F' and '8F' locomotives. No

92249 was built at Crewe in 1958, being first allocated to Ebbw Junction and withdrawn from Speke Junction in 1968. Seen here with a BR1G tender.
Colour-Rail/A. Sainty Collection (BRM1107)

Below:
No 92068 emerges out of Ashby Magna tunnel with a train of 16ton coal wagons in the evening sunlight in September 1964, its weather-beaten rusty form clashing with the autumn greenery of the cutting in the background. The locomotive was built at Crewe in 1955, first allocated to Doncaster and withdrawn from Derby in 1965. Seen here with a BR1F tender.
Colour-Rail//T. Tomalin (BRE1108)

Left:
Against a blue morning sky, No 92147 makes light work of its
heavy train of 16ton mineral wagons as it passes Little Wymondley
on 29 October 1961 with an up freight. This locomotive was built at
Crewe in 1957, first allocated to New England and withdrawn at
Immingham in 1965. Seen here with a BR1C tender.
Colour-Rail

Above:
In the afternoon sunshine No 92134 trundles a long train of mineral
wagons through Milbrook on 29 September 1961.
Colour-Rail

Above:
Building up steam at Carlisle Kingmoor, No 92166 in a clean condition for a '9F', in March 1961. This locomotive was one of the three '9Fs' fitted with the Berkley stokers when originally built, these eventually being removed during overhaul in the early 1960s. No 92166 was built at Crewe in 1958 and was allocated to Saltley during this period, being withdrawn from Birkenhead in 1967. It was fitted with a BR1K tender.

Right:
No 92013 eases past an outer home signal at Acocks Green in a summer sunset in 1965. No 92013 heads an unfitted train of coal in 16ton mineral wagons. Built at Crewe in 1954, it was first allocated to March and withdrawn from Saltley in 1966. Seen here with a BR1F tender.
M. Mensing

Left:
A dirty and rusty unidentified '9F' and BR tender passes Hatton in
1966, with a train of ore in a variety of hopper wagons.
M. Mensing

Above:
The same train ascending Hatton bank in rear view hauling a train of
hoppers in 1966.
M. Mensing

Left:
A dirty '9F' passes Knowle with a train of unfitted 16ton opens in 1965. No 92073 was built at Crewe in 1956, first allocated to Doncaster, and withdrawn from Birkenhead in 1967. Seen here with a BR1F tender.
M. Mensing

Right:
No 92151 accelerates away from Acocks Green in 1961 with a mixed freight train. No 92151 was built at Crewe in 1957 and first allocated to Saltley being withdrawn from Birkenhead in 1967. It is paired with a BR1C tender.
M. Mensing

Above:
No 92212 climbs the bank with a West Coast northbound heavy mineral train over Shap. This dramatic photograph shows a '9F' in full power thrashing its way to the summit complete with a banking locomotive at the rear in September 1967. Built at Swindon in 1959, first allocated to Banbury and withdrawn from Carnforth in 1968, No 92212 is seen here with a BR1G tender.
G. T. Robinson

Right:
Almost a year after steam locomotives had been withdrawn on the Southern Region, No 92203 makes its final journey in April 1968, southward from Crewe via London, to take its place as a working exhibit in a collection of preserved locomotives at the Longmoor Military Railway in Hampshire. Sadly, the project for a museum at Liss was abandoned in 1972. The locomotive was moved to Eastleigh, from where it was eventually to find a permanent home on the East Somerset Railway.
G. T. Robinson

Left:
No 92137, its cylinder cocks open, on shed at Carnforth in August 1967. This locomotive was built at Crewe in 1957, first allocated to Saltley and was finally withdrawn from Kingmoor in 1967. It is seen here with a BR1C tender.
G. T. Robinson

Below:
No 92223 with a train of iron ore hoppers in September 1966. This locomotive was built at Crewe in 1958, was first allocated to Banbury and finally withdrawn from Carnforth in 1968. Seen here with a BR1G tender.
G. T. Robinson

EVENING STAR

No 92220 BUILT AT SWINDON
MARCH 1960.
THE LAST STEAM LOCOMOTIVE FOR BRITISH RAILWAYS.
NAMED AT SWINDON ON MARCH 18? 1960 BY
K.W.C. GRAND ESQ.
MEMBER OF THE BRITISH TRANSPORT COMMISSION.

92220

Left inset:
The nameplate and plaque on the smoke deflector of *Evening Star* at Cardiff Canton shed on 17 March 1960, only days after the locomotive was named by Keith Grand at Swindon works.
C. J. Gammell

Left:
An interesting three-quarter view of *Evening Star* at Cardiff Canton shed on 17 March 1960. Soon after this photograph was taken, the green '9F' was put to work on Western Region passenger trains, including the 'Red Dragon'.
C. J. Gammell

Above:
No 92043 speeds its train of 16ton open wagons near Lutterworth in the autumn of 1964. This locomotive was built at Crewe in 1955, first allocated to March and finally withdrawn from Kingmoor in 1966. Seen here with a BR1F tender.
M. Mensing

Above:
Drifting through Solihull, Birmingham, No 92001 heads a mixed fitted freight in the late summer of 1961. The '9F' releases steam from its safety valves as it picks its way across the maze of points and slips outside the station.

62   *M. Mensing*

Right:
Heading a train of vans, No 92139 runs through Acocks Green in the summer of 1959. This locomotive was built at Crewe in 1957, first allocated to Saltley and finally withdrawn from Kingmoor in 1967. Seen here with a BR1C tender.
M. Mensing

Left:
An unidentified '9F' in the twilight, hauling a freight over Great Central metals near Rugby in 1963.
M. Mensing

Above:
'9F' No 92107 passes Sharnbrook in 1961 with a coal train. This four track section of the Midland main line was something of a galloping ground for these fine locomotives. No 92107 was built at Crewe in 1956, first allocated to Wellingborough and finally withdrawn from Birkenhead in 1967. Shown here paired with a BR1B tender. *M. Mensing*

No 92108 passes Charfield in 1965 with a train of mineral wagons.
This locomotive was built at Crewe in 1956 and first allocated to
Wellingborough, finally being withdrawn from Birkenhead in 1967.
Shown here with a BR1C tender.

M. Mensing

Evening Star on the Somerset & Dorset

With the warm evening sunshine glittering across its green painted form '9F' No 92220 *Evening Star* heads the 3.40pm Bournemouth-Bath near Wincanton in August 1962. Note the interesting formation of LMS Stanier carriage stock marshalled into short three and four-car sets. No 92220 was built at Swindon in 1960 and first allocated to Canton, being finally withdrawn from Cardiff East Dock in 1965. It is seen here with a BR1G tender.

Colour-Rail/J. G. Dewing(SD2)

Through the rolling hills and meadows, past grazing cows, and on its
way with the up 'Pines Express', No 92220 coasts down the grade
near Lyncombe Vale in September 1962. Again the carriage
formation is of interest with a neat rake of maroon Mk 1s, which
includes a Gresley buffet car in the centre.

Colour-Rail/W. Potter (SD144)

No 92220 in profile on a northbound express, near Cole in August
1962. This picture shows the clean lines of this beautiful machine to
good effect, with its impressive 10-coupled wheel arrangement and
lined green livery.
Colour-Rail/J. P. Mullett (SD162)

Crosti-boilered '9Fs'

Below:
Franco Crosti '9F' No 92020, at Wellingborough, awaiting cylinder repair in February 1960. This picture shows the original boiler and drafting arrangement to great effect; note the smoke deflector half-way down the boiler, which masks the steam exhaust arrangement. No 92020 was built at Crewe in 1955 and first allocated to Wellingborough, finally being withdrawn from Birkenhead in 1967. It is seen here with a BR1B tender.
Colour-Rail/D. H. Beecroft (BRM822)

Right:
A rare colour photograph of a Crosti '9F', No 92028, in use on heavy freight duty, shown here at Finedon Road in July 1959. A black smoke screen makes an impressive sight as it snakes its way out of the yard with a heavy coal train. This train consists of 16ton mineral wagons and 12ton eight plank open wagons. No 92028 was built at Crewe in 1955 and first allocated to Wellingborough, being finally withdrawn from Saltley in 1966. It is seen here with a BR1B tender.
Colour-Rail/K. H. C. Fairey(BRM615)

A rebuilt Crosti '9F' No 92020, seen in careworn condition at Stourton in June 1961. This fine picture shows the extent of rebuilding that has taken place with the removal of the side exhaust and external pipework, leaving a neater appearance.

Colour-Rail/C. J. B. Sanderson (BRM1362)

A shiny black ex-works rebuilt Crosti '9F', No 92029, at Kettering
on 29 August 1962, with drain cocks open as it stands in the sidings
between turns. Although the Crosti version had rather ugly features,
this photograph shows how impressive these machines could look.
No 92029 was built at Crewe in 1955 and first allocated to
Wellingborough, finally being withdrawn from Birkenhead in 1967.
Seen here with a BR1B tender.
Colour-Rail

Above:
A rebuilt Crosti locomotive No 92020 undergoing attention outside
Wellingborough shed on 8 July 1962. Some of these locomotives
were later transferred to the Birkenhead and Annersley areas, where
they worked until their withdrawal between 1966 and 1967.
Colour-Rail

Right:
Crosti '9F' No 92021 blasts its way through the snow near Warwick
with a long heavy coal train on 20 January 1963. This was during
the bad snowbound winter, which lasted until March of that year,
causing chaos on the railways.

Colour-Rail

Bluebell '9F'

Left:
Saved from oblivion, No 92240 undergoing restoration at Sheffield Park on the Bluebell Railway in Sussex. This locomotive was built at Crewe in 1958, first allocated to Ebbw Junction and was finally withdrawn from Southall in 1965. It ran with a BR1G tender.
C. J. Gammell

Right:
No 92240 in its element attacking Freshfield Bank in full power on the Bluebell Railway, shortly after its restoration. This fine photograph gives an impression of the power and strength of these beautiful and magnificent locomotives.
R. Ives

Locomotive Summary

No	Built	Withdrawn	First shed	Final shed	No	Built	Withdrawn	First shed	Final shed	No	Built	Withdrawn	First shed	Final shed
92000*	1/54	7/65	86A	85B	92057	10/55	10/65	18A	6C	92114	11/56	7/67	18B	68A
92001*	1/54	1/67	86A	56A	92058	10/55	11/67	18A	68A	92115	12/56	2/66	18B	8C
92002*	1/54	11/67	86A	6C	92059	10/55	9/66	18A	6C	92116	12/56	11/66	18B	8B
92003	1/54	3/65	86A	88B	92060	11/55	10/66	54B	54B	92117	12/56	12/67	18B	8C
92004	1/54	3/68	86A	11A	92061	11/55	9/66	54B	54B	92118	12/56	5/68	18B	11A
92005	2/54	8/65	86A	50A	92062	11/55	6/66	54B	54B	92119	2/57	9/67	18B	68A
92006*	2/54	4/67	86A	56A	92063	11/55	11/65	54B	54B	92120	2/57	7/67	18B	6C
92007	2/54	12/65	86A	85B	92064	12/55	11/66	54B	54B	92121	2/57	7/67	15A	6C
92008	3/54	10/67	15A	8B	92065	12/55	4/67	54B	56A	92122	2/57	11/67	15A	6C
92009	3/54	3/68	15A	11A	92066	12/55	5/65	54B	54B	92123	3/57	10/67	15A	6C
92010	5/54	4/66	31B	68A	92067	12/55	11/67	36A	84C	92124	3/57	12/66	15A	8B
92011	5/54	11/67	31B	6C	92068	12/55	1/66	36A	17A	92125	3/57	12/67	15A	68A
92012	5/54	10/67	31B	68A	92069	12/55	5/68	36A	8C	92126	3/57	8/67	15A	8B
92013	5/54	9/66	31B	21A	92070	1/56	11/67	36A	6C	92127	4/57	8/67	15A	6C
92014	5/54	10/67	31B	6C	92071	1/56	11/67	36A	68A	92128	4/57	11/67	18A	11A
92015	9/54	4/67	15A	68A	92072	2/56	1/66	36A	16B	92129	4/57	6/67	21A	68A
92016	10/54	10/67	15A	11A	92073	2/56	11/67	36A	6C	92130	4/57	5/66	21A	68A
92017	10/54	12/67	15A	68A	92074	2/56	4/67	36A	68A	92131	5/57	9/67	21A	6C
92018	10/54	4/67	15A	68A	92075	3/56	9/66	36A	68A	92132	5/57	10/67	21A	68A
92019	10/54	6/67	15A	68A	92076	3/56	2/67	36A	68A	92133	6/57	7/67	21A	6C
92020	5/55	10/67	15A	6C	92077	3/56	6/68	18A	11A	92134	6/57	12/66	21A	6C
92021	5/55	11/67	15A	6C	92078	3/56	5/67	18A	8B	92135	6/57	6/67	21A	56A
92022	5/55	11/67	15A	6C	92079*	4/56	11/67	18A	6C	92136	7/57	10/66	21A	21A
92023	5/55	11/67	15A	6C	92080	4/56	5/67	18A	68A	92137	7/57	9/67	21A	68A
92024	5/55	11/67	15A	6C	92081	5/56	2/66	18A	26A	92138	7/57	7/67	21A	8C
92025	6/55	11/67	15A	6C	92082	5/56	11/67	15A	6C	92139	7/57	9/67	21A	68A
92026	6/55	11/67	15A	6C	92083	5/56	2/67	15A	6C	92140	7/57	4/65	35A	40E
92027	6/55	8/67	15A	8C	92084	5/56	11/67	15A	6C	92141	12/57	12/65	35A	38A
92028	7/55	10/66	15A	21A	92085	6/56	12/66	15A	6C	92142	7/57	2/65	35A	35A
92029	7/55	11/67	15A	6C	92086	6/56	11/67	15A	6C	92143	8/57	2/65	35A	35A
92030	11/54	2/67	35A	56A	92087	8/56	2/67	36A	11A	92144	8/57	12/65	35A	38A
92031	11/54	1/67	31B	26A	92088	10/56	4/68	36A	11A	92145	8/57	2/66	35A	40B
92032	11/54	4/67	31B	6C	92089	9/56	2/67	36A	6C	92146	8/57	4/66	35A	36A
92033	11/54	9/65	31B	2E	92090	11/56	5/67	36A •	6C	92147	9/57	4/65	35A	40B
92034	12/54	5/64	35A	40B	92091	11/56	5/68	36A	11A	92148	9/57	12/65	35A	38A
92035	12/54	2/66	35A	40B	92092	11/56	10/66	36A	6C	92149	10/57	6/65	35A	40E
92036	12/54	12/64	35A	35A	92093	1/57	9/67	36A	68A	92150	10/57	4/67	18B	56A
92037	12/54	2/65	35A	40B	92094	2/57	5/68	36A	8C	92151	10/57	4/67	21A	6C
92038	12/54	4/65	35A	40E	92095	3/57	9/66	38B	8B	92152	10/57	11/67	21A	6C
92039	12/54	10/65	35A	40E	92096	4/57	2/67	38B	68A	92153	10/57	1/68	18A	8C
92040	12/54	8/65	35A	40E	92097	6/56	10/66	54B	54B	92154	10/57	7/67	15A	8C
92041	12/54	8/65	35A	40E	92098	7/57	7/66	54B	54B	92155	11/57	11/66	21A	8C
92042	1/55	12/65	35A	38A	92099	7/56	9/66	54B	54B	92156	11/57	7/67	18A	8B
92043	1/55	7/66	31B	68A	92100	8/56	5/67	18A	6C	92157	11/57	8/67	18A	6C
92044	1/55	4/65	31B	40E	92101	8/56	10/67	18A	6C	92158	11/57	7/66	18A	8C
92045	2/55	9/67	15A	6C	92102	8/56	11/67	18A	6C	92159	11/57	7/67	15A	6C
92046	2/55	10/67	15A	6C	92103	8/56	5/67	18A	6C	92160	11/57	6/68	15A	11A
92047	2/55	11/67	15A	6C	92104	8/56	2/67	18A	6C	92161	12/57	12/66	18B	68A
92048	2/55	9/67	15A	6C	92105	9/56	1/67	15A	6C	92162	12/57	11/67	18B	6C
92049	3/55	11/67	15A	6C	92106	9/56	7/67	15A	6C	92163	4/58	11/67	15B	6C
92050	9/55	9/67	18A	8B	92107	9/56	2/67	15A	6C	92164	4/58	7/66	15C	21A
92051	9/55	10/67	18A	68A	92108	10/56	11/67	15A	6C	92165*	4/58	3/68	21A	8C
92052	9/55	8/67	18A	68A	92109	10/56	11/67	18A	6C	92166*	5/58	11/67	21A	6C
92053	9/55	2/66	18A	8B	92110	10/56	12/67	18A	68A	92167*	5/58	6/68	21A	11A
92054	9/55	5/68	18A	8C	92111	11/56	10/67	14A	6C	92168	12/57	6/65	36A	36A
92055	9/55	12/67	18A	8C	92112	11/56	11/67	14A	6C	92169	12/57	5/65	36A	36A
92056	10/55	11/67	18A	68A	92113	11/56	10/67	18B	6C	92170	12/57	5/64	36A	36A

No	Built	Withdrawn	First shed	Final shed
92171	2/58	5/64	36A	35A
92172	1/58	4/66	36A	36A
92173	2/58	3/66	36A	36A
92174	2/58	12/65	36A	36A
92175	2/58	5/64	36A	36A
92176	3/58	5/64	36A	35A
92177	3/58	5/64	36A	36A
92178*	9/57	10/65	35A	40E
92179	10/57	11/65	35A	38A
92180	11/57	4/65	35A	40E
92181	11/57	2/65	35A	35A
92182	12/57	4/66	35A	36A
92183*	12/57	4/66	35A	36A
92184*	1/58	2/65	35A	40B
92185*	1/58	2/65	35A	40B
92186*	1/58	8/65	35A	40E
92187*	2/58	2/65	35A	38A
92188*	2/58	2/65	35A	38A
92189*	3/58	12/65	36B	38A
92190*	3/58	10/65	36B	36A
92191*	4/58	12/65	19A	38A
92192*	5/58	2/65	36A	36C
92193*	5/58	6/65	36A	40B
92194*	6/58	12/65	36A	40B
92195*	6/58	5/65	36A	40E
92196*	8/58	12/64	36A	40B
92197*	9/58	9/65	36A	40B
92198*	10/58	8/64	36A	36C
92199*	10/58	8/64	36A	36C
92200*	11/58	10/65	36A	40E
92201*	12/58	3/66	36A	36A
92202*	12/58	12/65	36A	40B
92203*	4/59	11/67	82B	6C
92204*	4/59	12/67	82B	8C
92205*	5/59	6/67	82B	56A
92206*	5/59	5/67	82B	56A
92207*	6/59	12/64	82B	86A
92208*	6/59	10/67	83D	68A
92209*	6/59	12/65	83D	71G
92210*	8/59	11/64	86C	86A
92211*	9/59	5/67	81A	56A
92212*	9/59	1/68	84C	11A
92213*	10/59	11/66	82B	84C
92214*	10/59	8/65	86C	86E
92215*	11/59	6/67	84C	56A
92216*	12/59	10/65	86C	86E
92217*	12/59	7/66	86C	84E
92218*	1/60	5/68	82B	8C
92219*	1/60	8/65	82B	88B
92220*	3/60	3/65	86C	88B
92221*	5/58	5/65	84C	50A
92222*	6/58	3/65	84C	81C
92223*	6/58	4/68	84C	11A
92224*	6/58	9/67	84C	8B
92225*	6/58	7/65	84C	86A
92226*	6/58	9/65	84C	86E
92227*	7/58	11/67	84C	8C
92228*	7/58	1/67	84C	8C
92229*	7/58	11/64	84C	86A
92230*	8/58	12/65	84C	85B
92231*	8/58	11/66	86G	50A
92232*	8/58	12/64	86G	88B
92233*	8/58	2/68	86G	8C
92234*	8/58	11/67	86G	6C
92235*	8/58	11/65	86G	82A
92236*	9/58	4/65	86G	86E
92237*	9/58	6/65	86A	86A
92238*	9/58	9/65	86A	86E
92239*	9/58	11/66	86A	50A
92240*	10/58	8/65	86A	81C
92241*	10/58	7/65	86A	81C
92242*	10/58	5/65	86A	86E
92243*	10/58	12/65	86A	71G
92244*	11/58	12/65	86A	85B
92245*	11/58	12/64	81A	81C
92246*	12/58	12/65	81A	85B
92247*	12/58	10/66	81A	26A
92248*	12/58	5/65	86A	88B
92249*	12/58	5/68	86A	8C
92250†	12/58	12/65	84C	85B

*Fitted with double chimney
† Fitted with Giesl ejector

Locomotive notes
92020-9 fitted with Crosti boiler, Crosti preheater later sealed off.
92097-9 fitted with air compressors for working Tyne Dock-Consett iron ore trains.
92165-7 fitted with Berkley mechanical stokers.

Building details
92000-14 built at Crewe, order No E487
92015-19 built at Crewe, order No E491
92020-29 built at Crewe, order No E488
92030-49 built at Crewe, order No E489
92050-86 built at Crewe, order No E490
92087-96 built at Swindon, lot No 421
92097-134 built at Crewe, order No E493
92135-177 built at Crewe, order No E494
92178-202 built at Swindon, lot No 487
92203-220 built at Swindon, lot No 429
92221-250 built at Crewe, order No E497

Shed codes
The codes listed here are those in use during 1957.

2E	Northampton
6C	Birkenhead
8B	Warrington
8C	Speke Junction
11A	Carnforth
14A	Cricklewood
15A	Wellingborough
15B	Kettering
15C	Leicester
16B	Kirkby-in-Ashfield
17A	Derby
18A	Toton
18B	Westhouses
19A	Sheffield Darnall
21A	Saltley
26A	Newton Heath
31B	March
35A	New England
36A	Doncaster
36B	Mexborough
36C	Frodingham
38A	Colwick
38B	Annesley
40B	Immingham
40E	Langwith
50A	York
54B	Tyne Dock
56A	Wakefield
68A	Carlisle Kingmoor
71G	Bath Green Park
81A	Old Oak Common
81C	Southall
82A	Bristol, Barrow Road
82B	Bristol, St Philip's Marsh
83D	Laira
84C	Banbury
84E	Tyseley
85B	Gloucester
86A	Newport Ebbw Vale
86C	Cardiff Canton
86E	Severn Tunnel Junction
86G	Pontypool Road

Left:
Evening Star, again at Cole, on 18 August 1962, with the 3.40pm
Bournemouth-Bath, its rake of LMS stock bathed in sunshine as the
train crosses Cole Viaduct. *Colour-Rail*

Above:
A grubby unidentified '9F' heads a fitted van train over Lapworth
troughs in the summer of 1966. Note the large water tank supplying
the troughs on the left.
M. Mensing

Back cover:
A '9F' doing what it was designed for — hauling heavy long-
distance freight. No 92030 is seen trundling through the countryside
with a rake of ironstone hoppers in tow. *M. Mensing*

Afterword

What a deplorable waste it all was and it was all in the name of progress.

In the mid-1960s, hundreds of almost brand new steam locomotives were prematurely thrown on the scrap head in a frenzy of dieselisation. My BR Standard '9F' locomotive, No 92203, which I subsequently named *Black Prince*, is surely a supreme example of this highly questionable philosophy. She cost almost £60,000 to build, in 1959, and just eight years later, in full working order, I paid £3,000 for her.

Our great steam age did not go out in a blaze of glory as it should have done, after nearly 140 years. It went out in scenes of squalor and degradation. Locomotives were anonymous, with their number plates removed or stolen, and the cab side numbers under layers of grime and filth. The diesel represented the shiny new age of progress and we had to get rid of steam as quickly as possible at all costs — and what a cost. We were throwing away locomotives which burned British coal to replace them with oil which we had to buy from abroad; we didn't have North Sea Oil in those days!

I am not in the least mechanically minded. I know nothing about the mechanical workings of an engine. I just love them as subjects to paint and subjects to stir the emotions; they are alive, as everyone who knows a steam engine will agree.

My venture into preservation began with a phone call, in 1967. Being impetuous by nature, and with scarcely a thought for what I was doing, I telephoned an influential friend in British Rail and said, 'Bob, I want to buy two steam engines'.

(I purchased No 75029, a BR Standard '4', which I subsequently named *The Green Knight*, as well.)

At least I had the sense on that phone call to say, 'I want a good one — I don't want a junk one which is going to be thrown away for scrap'. British Rail were really awfully good about it. They said, 'Well, you can have 92203. She has just been "done up" for the last steam-hauled freight run from Liverpool Docks to the Shotton Steel Works on The Wirral'. As a result of that phone call, I found myself the bewildered and rather frightened owner of two locomotives weighing over 130 tons each, both almost new; and neither of them has ever been near a scrap yard.

Although I did not know it at the time, the project which was ultimately to become the East Somerset Railway was born as a result of that telephone call, but that is another story.

It is a sobering thought, suffice to say, that I have now owned *Black Prince* for more than three times her working life on British Rail. Furthermore, she has just completed an overhaul which has cost many times the price paid for her in the first place. Nevertheless, we believe that steam locomotives are worth preserving. They may belong to a more leisurely and romantic age but this fact alone surely justified their preservation in full working order for the enjoyment and enlightenment of young people growing up in a modern world which does not bother as much as it should about the great inventions of the past. We also believe that they will give pleasure to those who like to look back and remember.

David Shepherd